ROADS RAILWAYS AND CANALS

Mark C.W. Sleep

Wayland

YOUNG EXPLORER

Acknowledgements

The photographs in this book were supplied by: British
Tourist Authority 10 (left); Bruce Coleman Limited/
Wayland Picture Library 14; Alan Hutchison Library 23/
Bernard Régent 9, 13; International Society for Educational
Information Inc. 31; P. J. Howard/Millbrook House 26, 27, 28;
TOPHAM 12, 20, 21; Wayland Picture Library 10 (right), 30.

First published in 1983 by Wayland Publishers Limited
49 Lansdowne Place, Hove, East Sussex BN3 1HF, England
© Copyright 1983 Wayland Publishers Limited

ISBN 0 85078 275 9

Illustrated and designed by John Yates
Typeset by The Grange Press, Butts Road, Southwick, Sussex
Printed in Italy by G. Canale & C.S.p.A., Turin

Contents

In the country

Visit a minor country road near you. How is it bordered – by fences, walls, hedges, railings, posts, trees or ditches?

Is there a pavement – on one side, both sides, or not at all?

Stand at various positions along the road and estimate how far you can see in each direction. Make sure that there is no traffic coming, and then pace the width of the road.

How is the land used on either side of the road? Is the road's surface clean? If not, what is dirtying it?

Try to find out when the buildings served by this road were built. How old do you think the road is? What do you think is the average speed of private cars using the road?

Carry out a traffic survey on your country road. Try to do one between 8 a.m. and 9 a.m. Repeat it for an hour between 11 a.m. and 3 p.m. and for a final hour between 5 p.m. and 7 p.m., before dark.

Record your information under the following headings:

	Number of vehicles/pedestrians travelling					
	From A to B 8 a.m.-9 a.m.	From B to A 8 a.m.-9 a.m.	From A to B 11a.m.-12a.m.	From B to A 11a.m.-12a.m.	From A to B 6 p.m.-7 p.m.	From B to A 6 p.m.-7 p.m.
Pedestrians						
Cyclists						
Private cars						
Mopeds & Motorbikes						
Vans						
Trucks						
Buses/ Coaches						
Farm vehicles						
Emergency services' vehicles						

You may need one or two friends to help you to collect this information, but if it is a quiet country road, you can probably do it by yourself. Prepare a large copy of this chart and put single ticks for each passing vehicle or pedestrian. At the end of the period, add up the ticks and circle the totals.

Compare a weekday survey with a Saturday and a Sunday survey. Can you explain the differences throughout the day and between days?

Near towns and cities

Visit one of the busy major roads on the edge of your nearest town or city. Ask yourself all the questions on page 4.

Using safe places to cross, such as traffic lights, foot-bridges or pedestrian crossings, pace the width of the road.

Now repeat your traffic surveys for the same times and days of the week as you did for the country road. This might be very difficult by yourself, so you must either get some school friends to help you; or you must take some sample figures for, say, 5 or 10 minute intervals in one or two categories at a time, and then multiply these figures up to make 1 hour readings.

Try to explain the main differences that emerge from your surveys of a country road and a major road.

Here are some further ways in which minor country roads and major city roads may differ from each other:

Advertising boards, drains, road signs, street lights, dual carriageways, traffic lights, houses at roadside, shops at roadside, bus stops, telephone and electricity cables, side streets, delivery vans, road surfaces, road thicknesses (as seen during repair work), litter bins.

Can you think of any others? Look at the drawing for some help.

What do you see as the major problems concerning city roads and their users?

Between major towns and cities

View a local motorway or freeway either from a foot-bridge or from the footpath of a road that crosses it.

Observe and record all the information that was requested for country roads and major roads. Never go on to a motorway, but always take your readings from points of safety.

What are the most important differences between the set of results for a motorway and those obtained for a country road and a major city road?

From the information that you have gained about your three routeways, complete the following table:

	Country road	Major road	Motorway
Total width from boundary fence to boundary fence			
Total width of tarmac used by traffic			
Number of traffic lanes in each direction			
Average width of each traffic lane			
Pavements (numbers, width)			
Number of private cars per hour			
Estimated average speed of private cars			
Suggested date of road's construction			

When motorways meet, complicated flyovers are built, like the ones below, which take up a lot of space. Why do you think flyovers are used instead of roundabouts or cross-roads with traffic lights?

Roads in towns

Try to collect old pictures or postcards of your town, or visit the nearest town or city that still has some old streets. How do the streets differ from those of today.

Are they wider or narrower?

Are they made of the same materials as the streets of today? If not, of what materials are they made?

Are there any cobbled streets?

From the old pictures, can you see any street lights?

Now visit a modern shopping precinct. Is the traffic allowed into the main shopping area? Are there any covered walkways to prevent you getting wet while you are going from shop to shop?

At night, how would a modern city street compare with a city street of a few hundred years ago?

Road networks

Look at a map of your country showing the major road networks. Can you detect any pattern in the networks or are the roads arranged higgledy-piggledy? Do the roads appear to radiate from the major towns?

Now look at a large-scale map of your area. How are the different sorts of roads shown?

How do roads cross ranges of hills or mountains?

Few road vehicles can climb gradients of more than 1 in 3. How have road engineers overcome this problem?

Are there any towns in your area that have no roads leading to them?

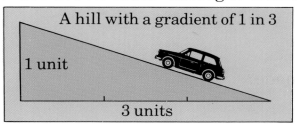

A hill with a gradient of 1 in 3

1 unit

3 units

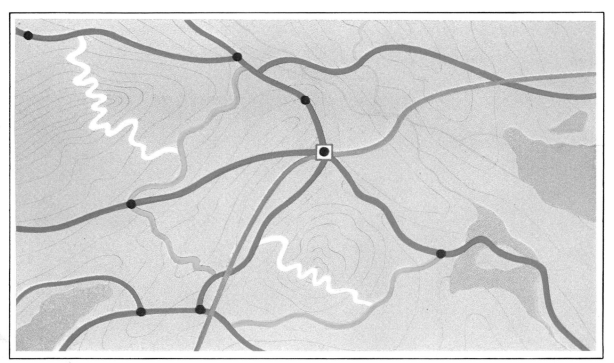

11

Roads and the environment

Many people travel by car because it is more convenient. It is also often the quickest and cheapest way to travel. There are obvious advantages, but what about the disadvantages? Look at the picture below.

Repeat your major road survey for private cars only. How many cars have only a driver and no passengers?

Now look at this table.

	Miles per gallon of fuel	Number of persons carried	Cost in gallons per mile per head
Car with driver only	30	1	0.033
Bus	10	80	0.00125
Diesel train	1	800	0.00125

How much more wasteful of fuel is a car with one occupant than a full bus or train?

From the table (left), we can see that 800 private cars each carrying 1 person equals 10 buses carrying 80 persons each, which equals a single train carrying 800 passengers. Which means of transport will pollute the atmosphere the most? The photograph below shows the polluted atmosphere above Los Angeles, USA.

Try to find out the annual accident figures in your area for road and rail transport. Which is the safest form of transport, and therefore the cheapest in terms of the cost of accidents?

Ask at your local police station where some of the local accident 'black spots' are. Visit one during a rush hour. Stand well back from the kerb so that you do not add to the hazard by blocking the view of drivers. Observe the problems that occur. How could some of these problems be solved? Do you think that this would be expensive?

Heavy goods vehicles

Roads are as important for carrying goods as they are for carrying passengers. Door-to-door service by truck usually means quicker and cheaper deliveries, and this is good for the customer.

But there are disadvantages. Stand by any roadside and wait for a heavy truck to pass you. What do you notice about the noise?

Now close your eyes and plug your ears. Can you still tell when a heavy truck is passing? How did you know?

Look at the table below and see how much damage heavy trucks are doing to the roads and the surrounding buildings compared with a car.

	Total environmental damage
1-tonne family car on 2 axles	1 unit
10-tonne truck on 2 axles	10,000 units
20-tonne truck on 2 axles	160,000 units

2. Early transport

Ancient roads and trackways

The earliest roads were built by the ancient civilizations of the Middle East and the Mediterranean areas about 2,500 years ago. Find out the names of some of the peoples who lived in these parts of the world.

Many ancient cities had beautiful paved streets. The cities were linked by long, usually unpaved, roads. Why did the roads not need to be paved?

The early roads were used for trade and for administration purposes. What other important uses did ancient civilizations have for roads?

The earliest roads in North America were the narrow foot trails of the Indians. The Indians were hunters and their paths followed the movements of deer, elk, and buffalo.

Ancient European roads were often built along river valleys or along spring lines. What is a spring line? What are the advantages of building roads along river valleys and spring lines? Are roads still built along river valleys?

Roman roads

The Romans, who ruled most of Europe from before the birth of Christ until about AD 500, were the finest early road-builders. Their roads were carefully planned and engineered. They had solid foundations and they were built as nearly as possible in a straight line.

What are the advantages of building straight roads?

Try to find out the names of Roman roads that are still in use in Britain and Europe today.

Look at the map below of the roads of Roman Europe. Why was it so important for the Romans to have a fast and efficient transport system?

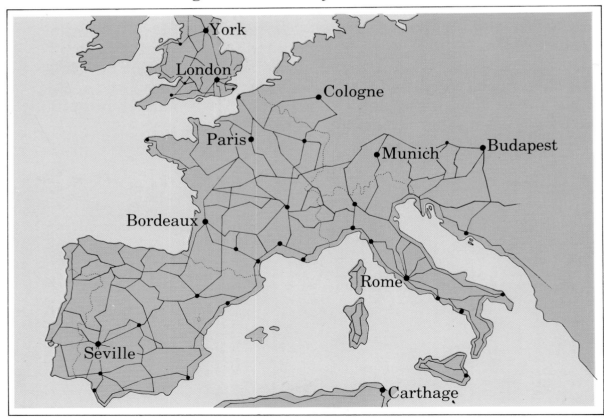

Other early transport routes

In mountainous areas, in forested country, in desert regions and in marshy swampland, an important form of early transport was by river.

What are the hazards and problems of travelling along rivers?

The cheapest and often the quickest way of moving people and goods from place to place in a country was around the coast by sea. Before 1800, many of the most important towns and cities of the world were ports. Is this true of the towns and cities of your country?

Primitive forms of transport today

In poor countries and in countries that are thinly populated, there are few roads, canals or railways. Why is this? People in these countries often rely on primitive means of transport to move themselves and their goods around the country.

Human porters are still used in wet, tropical countries and in countries where human labour is cheap. Find out in what countries human porters are used to carry goods.

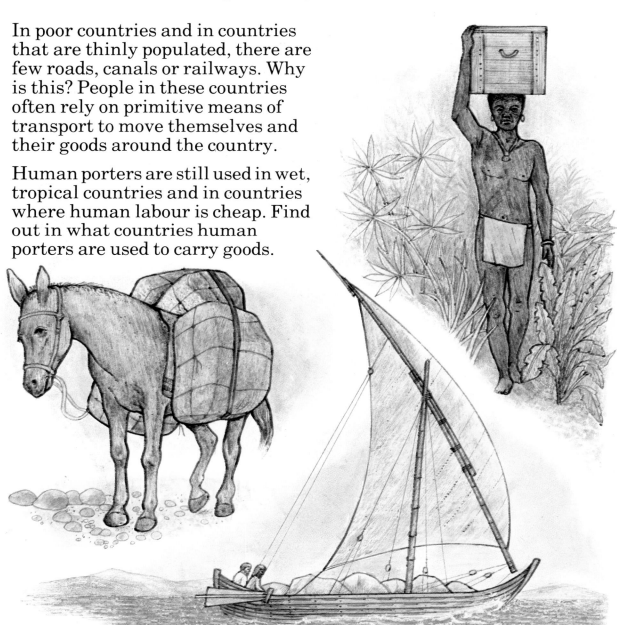

18

Pack animals, such as mules, are used for carrying goods in dry, rugged countries, while camels are used in the desert. Find out the countries where mules and camels are still used. What other pack animals are there? In what countries are they used?

Draught animals are those that pull carts and sleds. What are the advantages of draught animals over pack animals, and in which areas of the world are they used?

Primitive boats are still used in some remote river areas. In which river areas are primitive boats still in use? Dhows are still used in some Middle Eastern countries. What is a dhow?

3. Canals and river transport

Why build canals?

Water transport is basically the cheapest form of transport. Canals are waterways which Man has built to make the best possible use of this cheap form of transport.

Canals may be built to link two seas or oceans together and so save travelling time.

In your atlas, look up the Panama (shown below), Suez, Kiel, Caledonian and Corinth canals and calculate the distances saved by each of these waterways. Find out when they were built.

Man has also built canals to carry heavy loads inland. A barge carrying many tonnes of clay, timber, slates, coal, iron ore, or sand could easily be pulled by a single horse from a towpath. The same quantity would have needed hundreds of loads with a horse and cart.

The age of canals

During the early years of the Industrial Revolution in the late eighteenth century, thousands of miles of canals were built in Europe and elsewhere in the world.

Many rivers were also canalized for water transport. With the invention of the steam-engine, barges were adapted to steam.

The canals continued to be busy in spite of the huge increase in traffic being taken by the railways. Can you think why this was so?

Huge aqueducts, like the one below, had to be built to take the canals across ravines and valleys.

Long tunnels were also built to take the barges through hills. It was impossible to take horses on towpaths through these tunnels, so the barges had to 'leg it'. See if you can visit a canal tunnel and see the foot prints on the roof or sides for yourself.

With the invention of the internal combustion engine in the nineteenth century, powerful diesel engines were used to drive barges and tugs along the waterways of the world.

Locks and water supplies

The two great problems that canal builders had to overcome were the changes in the height of the land and the need for a constant supply of water.

The first problem was usually overcome with the use of locks. Try to visit a lock on a canal or river near you. From the picture below, work out the sequence of events that is necessary to move a boat up-or downstream through the lock.

The water problem was usually overcome by diverting part of a local river into the newly built canal. Often a control lake or reservoir would dam up sufficient water to last the summer and sluice gates would then be used to supply the canal with water.

A second method was to canalize parts of a river bed. In this way the cost was minimized and a water supply was assured.

Is there a canalized river near you?

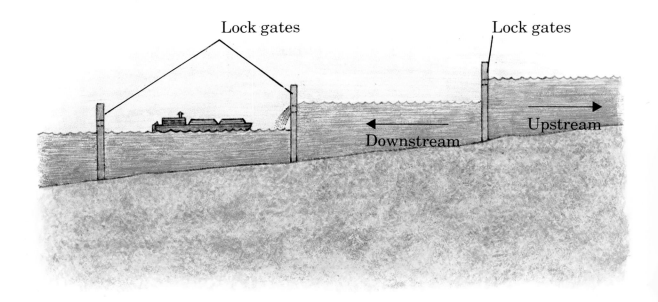

On an outline map of the world, mark in and label the important ship canals mentioned on page 20 and the following inland waterways:

The Great Lakes of North America, with the Sault Ste. Marie, St. Clair and Welland canals; the St. Lawrence waterway, Canada; the Erie canal and the Hudson-Mohawk river link, USA; the river Mississippi-Missouri, USA; the river Amazon, South America; the river Rhine (shown below) of Germany and Holland; the river Danube and the Oder-Danube canal in Europe; the Göta canal, Sweden; the Volga-Moscow canal, the White Sea canal, the Volga-Don canal, all in the USSR; the Mittelland canal, the river Ruhr, the Dortmund-Ems canal, the river Elbe, all in West Germany; the river Schelde, Belgium.

Bridges

Canals and canalized rivers were built to serve industry and therefore industrial areas of dense population. In these areas, roads, railways, trackways and footpaths have to cross over or under the waterways.

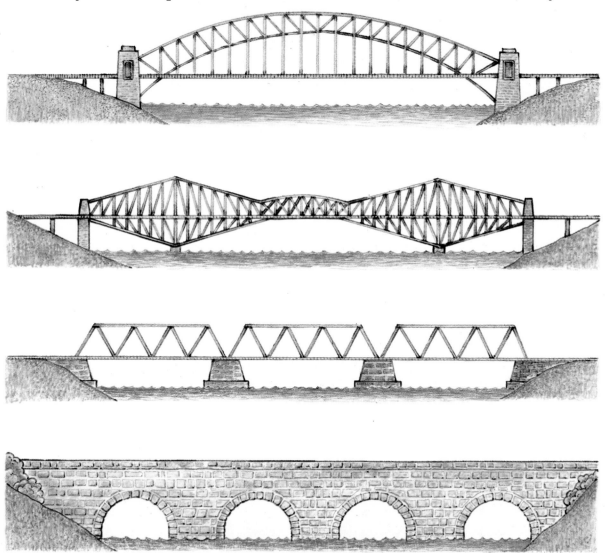

Visit your nearest river or canal town and see how many different types of bridges you can find.

Draw sketches of the different types. Can you name the different types of bridges shown here?

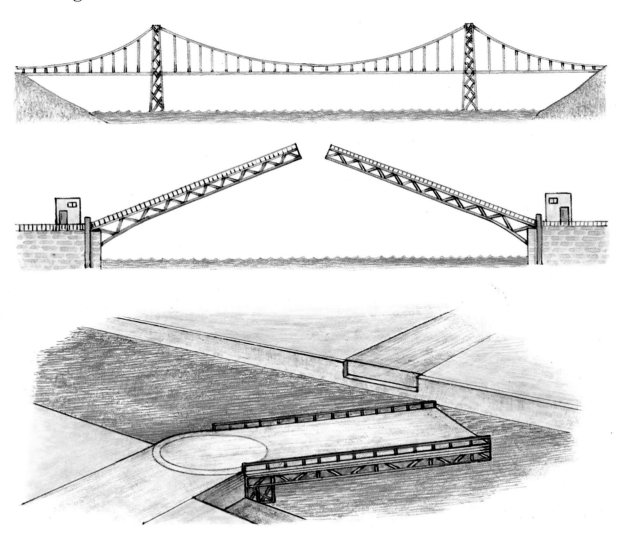

4. Railway transport

Your local track

Visit a bridge over your nearest busy railway line and record your answers to the following questions.

What type of bridge is it? How many tracks are there beneath it? (one track is a pair of lines carrying one train.) Are some tracks used for fast trains and others for slow trains?

Do trains always travel in the same direction on the same track? What is the total width of the land owned by the railway company? Pace the distance from fence to fence across the bridge.

How far can you see in each direction along the track from your bridge? Are the trains diesel, steam or electrically powered? If they are electrically driven, how do the trains pick up the electricity?

What sort of trains use the track — local trains with only a few carriages, goods trains, or express trains with many carriages? What is carried in the goods trains? Do different types of trains use the track at different times of the day?

Find out the average speed of the trains that pass under your bridge. You can do this by measuring on a map the distance from your bridge to the next bridge or road crossing. Time the train between the two points in seconds and work out the speed.

Are all the various types of trains doing similar speeds in each direction? If not, why do you think that they are different?

Your local station

Visit the railway station of your nearest large town and buy a platform ticket. How many platforms are there?

Look up the train timetable and find out how many trains go to various destinations each day.

By finding out how many people can be carried in a railway carriage and the number of carriages on each train, calculate how many people could be carried daily to each destination if the trains were full.

Find out the travel time and cost to get from your local station to the next main town. Would it be cheaper or quicker by car?

How many people would have to go in one car to make it cheaper per person than by rail?

Are rail prices the same for all times of the day and for all times of the year?

Railway networks

Look at a map of your country showing the major railway networks. Can you detect any pattern in the network? Do most of the railway lines seem to radiate from one or two major cities? Do most of the lines seem to run in any particular direction?

Are there any major towns or cities in your country that are not on the railway?

Now look at a large-scale map of your area. How are the railways shown? What routes do they follow? What happens when a railway line has to cross over a range of hills?

Few railway trains can climb gradients of over 1 in 30. How have railway engineers overcome this problem?

How are embankments, cuttings, tunnels and road crossings shown on your map?

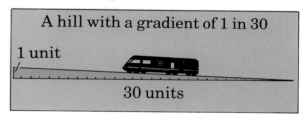

A hill with a gradient of 1 in 30

1 unit

30 units

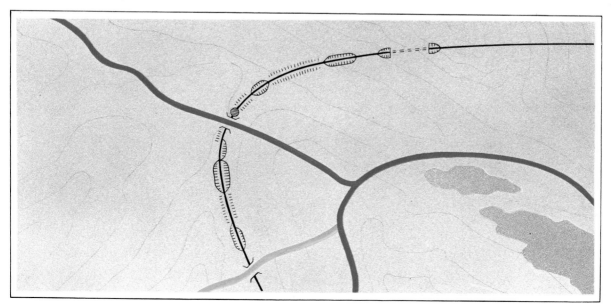

Railways of the past

What great advantages do you think the early railways of the nineteenth century had over the horse and cart and the canals? As the years passed, why do you think that these advantages became greater and greater? By the end of the nineteenth century, a railway network covered most of the industrial countries of the world and linked almost all the major cities. Transcontinental railways stretched across North America, Europe, Africa, Australia and Asia and opened up vast areas of farmland and large mineral reserves. Railways were even constructed to go up mountains and down mines.

Look at old maps of your country and notice how the rail networks grew between 1830 and 1900.

Find out as much as you can about these early railways – their different gauges and their various means of locomotion.

If there is a railway museum in your country, it will probably be a very worthwhile visit.

Railways of today and tomorrow

The beginning of the twentieth century saw railway networks linking even the smallest villages in some countries. However, just as the railways had taken business away from the canals at the beginning of the nineteenth century, so the internal combustion engine had a profound effect upon the railways in the twentieth century.

Motor coaches, trucks and cars slowly took over from trains. Can you think of their obvious advantages, especially for pleasure purposes and short journeys? Up to the present day, for longer journeys and for heavy goods, the railways have generally continued to win the bulk of the traffic. However, as we saw in Chapter 1, heavy goods trucks provide a door-to-door service.

In what form do you see the railways surviving if this trend continues in the future?

Index

Glossary

Administration   Matters connected with the running of a country.
Gauge   The distance between the rails of a railway track.
Gradient   The amount of slope in a road or railway.
'Legging it'   To move a boat through a tunnel by lying on your back and pushing against the tunnel's roof or sides with your feet.
Pollute   To make dirty.
Primitive   Of very early times.